THE UNIVERSITY OF
WINCHESTER

Martial Rose Library
Tel: 01962 827306

_ 4 NOV 2008

To be returned on or before t

D1348777

HANS WERNER HENZE

ONDINE

DIARY OF A BALLET

HANS WERNER HENZE

ONDINE

DIARY OF A BALLET

Preface by Alfred Andersch
Translated by Daniel Pashley

DANCE BOOKS

First published in Germany. © R. Piper & Co Verlag, Munich, 1959.

First published in English in 2003 by Dance Books Ltd, 4 Lenten Street, Alton,
Hampshire GU34 1HG

Printed by H. Charlesworth & Co., Huddersfield

ISBN: 1 85273 095 1

For my brother Jürgen

Illustrations

The photographs are by Roger Wood. The other illustrations are derived from costume designs and scene sketches by Lila de Nobili.

PREFACE

Henze's *Diary of a Ballet* is an exact record of the preparation of a work of art. Written records of this kind are so rare, especially in Germany, that accomplished examples must be counted among the greatest treasures of creative work.

When dealing with an art form as complicated as ballet, where, as with cinema, the final production is the result of the efforts of an artistic ensemble, the difficulties involved in describing oneself can become immense. The genius wrestling alone with the poem, novel, drama, symphony or picture is depicted easily enough. But how is one to describe the momentum of a company; the composer, the choreographer, the stage designer, the *prima ballerina assoluta*?

Henze has not merely contented himself with providing a description of the practical organisation of a ballet, fascinating as these parts of his diary are. He lays open for us the kernel from which the piece develops, giving us the history of an idea and its translation into a visual representation. The ways in which milieu, atmosphere and thought must unite to produce art will become clear to us as we read. Technical notes on the composition intermingle constantly with Neapolitan street scenes; precise timing instructions with elegies to swans on the Thames; careful considerations about how best to interpret the figure of Ondine with precious frivolity; refinement with spontaneity; feeling with the organisation of feeling; being with awareness of being. We are looking into the sorcerer's kitchen.

The account of the individual work sheds light on what today one terms the 'situation of modern art'. These parts of the diary may – and should – give rise to the greatest controversy. I do not share Henze's views on the effects of Bauhaus and abstract art on the stage. He mistakes Bauhaus for the terror of those dogmatists upon whom today's audiences have conferred the role of an officially recognised avant-garde. The masters of Bauhaus have nothing in common with these self-righteous young augurs; rather, they were just as upright, spontaneous, open and unprovincial as the creator of this new *Ondine* and of the diary that is accompanying its apparition.

Enough. I have already gone too far in interpreting something that is self-explanatory. Did I use the term exact record? As someone who works hard to write narrative prose, I must remark with a certain amount of professional envy that a composer – a literary outsider, therefore – has succeeded in writing a miniature novel presenting the birth of a work of art as the interplay of people and forms. A miniature novel – that is truly something great.

Hamburg, September 1959
Alfred Andersch

...to accept space, to own
That surfaces need not be superficial
Nor gestures vulgar, cannot really
Be taught within earshot of running water
Or in sight of a cloud.
(Wystan H. Auden: *Good-bye to the Mezzogiorno*)

The first discussions about *Ondine* took place in Forio on Ischia. The focal point of this village was 'Maria Internazionale', the owner of a café whose chairs and tables had to be extended far out over the piazza on summer evenings, in order to accommodate the many Neapolitan families and the foreign poets and painters who would meet here for an aperitif or for midnight conversations that would stretch on until dawn. Maria Internazionale had offered the use of her home to Frederick Ashton, the choreographer and artistic director of the Royal Ballet, who had arrived in time for the start of the San Vito Festival. It was relatively cool there, and offered partial protection from the noise of the festival. But I remember that one of the many bells that rang at the most astonishing hours of the day – wildly and enduringly – was quite nearby, and managed to silence all discussion about *Ondine* for a quarter of an hour.

I myself, having crossed from Naples, had a room in a farmhouse in the vineyards of San Francesco, but had to walk into the village when I wanted to work with Ashton. In an almost empty, whitewashed room we sat opposite one another and tried to keep our first sketches together in school exercise books. The story by de la Motte-Fouqué was to be our basis. It had also inspired the *Ondine* ballet of the nineteenth century and served as a source for Giraudoux's drama.

The book, decorated by Arthur Rackham, translated by W.L. Courtney and published in 1909, was one that Ashton had with him from morning to night, including when he was on the beach. There it became sandy and salty, the sun causing it to become ever more warped, as if hinting at the later development of our *Ondine*. It was difficult to sketch out a simple, linear story from the complex narrative with its extremely exacting details, let alone represent this story in dance, or in danceable ideas. The simpler and more straightforward the story, the easier it would be for us to represent it in pure choreographic forms.

An early suggestion was the idea of showing every thought in absolute dance, thereby completely eliminating all elements of mime – that explanatory, communicative medium with its frozen rituals. But it soon became clear that this would not be possible, and in the case of a three-act work – enough for a full evening – not at all desirable. So mime was brought in here and there, effective precisely because of its rather old-fashioned formality in the eyes of today's audiences: short, fleeting communications with the audience, enabling them to fly all the more freely off into the pure fantasy world of absolute dance.

In night-time piazza conversations, our literary friends displayed very particular ideas of *their Ondine*: classical, baroque, mystical, surrealist, functional, expressionist or neo-romantic ('and in the background, lit yellow by the moon and torches, the façades of the houses with their rustic bow windows, the shadow of an opera backdrop…'). Refusing to let ourselves be beaten down, we pressed on towards a first draft, still very fragmented, still very close to Fouqué's territory.

Act I

Pastoral sea scene, fishermen mending their nets. We see a hermit. After sunset everything becomes sinister; the forest changes, Knight Huldbrand appears, and as he crosses the forest he is greatly disturbed by ghosts and sinister apparitions. He comes to a hut and is let in. Ondine, the adopted daughter of the fishing folk who live in the hut, comes in, falls in love with Huldbrand, asks for an amulet that Huldbrand is wearing. He refuses. She runs away. Huldbrand follows her.

Will-o'-the-wisps in the forest; Huldbrand surrounded by Ondines who are confusing him. At last he manages to capture his Ondine and carry her to the hut. Marriage the next morning, with the hermit officiating, in the presence of the village folk.

Act II

On a ship, a pleasure cruise or a celebration. The hostess is Bertalda. She falls in love with Huldbrand, who falls equally in love with her, while Ondine's supernatural playing with the waves and the wind makes her appear sinister to him. Eventually he takes no more notice of her, and as he offers Bertalda the amulet that he refused to give to Ondine, Ondine returns to her siblings in the sea. Kühleborn, the angry uncle (father), King of the Mediterranean, commands a storm in which the ship sinks.

Act III Notes missing.

These basic words and rough plotlines were lacking in all subtlety and in particular in a thought-through interpretation of the Ondine idea, which is almost a myth. Would we be successful in transferring what is essentially a literary idea into absolute theatre? At this initial point we were still too close to Fouqué and therefore at the same time very far away from his story, far from its magic, its gracious hardship and pain. Apparently the

Ondine, costume design

actual setting imagined for this love story (an autobiographical one, as I learnt from Arno Schmidt) was in North Germany at the Steinhuder Sea and on the banks of the Weser. Upon reading the story, one is transported to the cool, moss-covered Black Forest with a deep, clear lake, and one follows the lovers on their boat trip down the Danube to Vienna.

In the chalk-white room of a Mediterranean fishing village among houses from Turkish times, *palazzi* in rustic Spanish baroque, set against the shrill tone of the *cicada* at midday, when the sky turns white with heat and the inky blue of the sea seems to dissolve in a haze at the horizon, all ideas of a shady German forest, rainy marshland and cool lakes were very pleasant, but quite unreal and vague... Stories of Ondine, salamanders and elements of the secret land of cool waters made up the preferred literature of Adrian Leverkühn, as the flames of hell started to lick towards him; and Proust in the first volume of his *Recherche* read about water and dampness during hot days in Balbec in order to keep cool. But it was the time of the San Vito Festival, shortly before *ferragosta*, and the bells were striking suddenly and at length. Early-morning gun salutes were being fired in the harbour to welcome the village's famous sons on their arrival, among them a deceased Cardinal in his coffin.

In the main streets, market stalls had been set up – melon sellers, pastry bakers, puppet shows – and on the piazza stood a white-golden pavilion in which the *banda*, a rough brass band, played for several hours each evening. The sextet from *Lucia di Lammermoor*, or 'Ballet music and triumphant march from *Aida*' were scarcely able, despite sustained *fortissimi*, to overcome the festive noise coming from the participants themselves. Everyone was gripped with the joy that comes from carefree, almost heathen pleasures, and the reality of the festival and the country took root in our *Ondine*, at first imperceptibly, but soon very visibly. Sounds and colours, movements and gestures, qualities of light and shade and moments made their way into the musical consciousness and also the imagination of the choreographer.

He had in fact come from Gothic England with a preset idea. This seemed now to be changing, on the one hand because of my 'continental' ideas about ballet and the art of ballet music, on the other – by far the most convincing factor – because of this magnificent Mediterranean summer. On one of the evenings of the festival (which, once started, would not stop for a week) the builders had erected petroleum lamps in honour of Saint Francesco on the hill bearing his name and along the mole. The lamps flickered yellow and gave off a sooty smoke, a seemingly heathen fire, like faunish guiding stars or will-o'-the-wisps.

What is Ondine? Who is Ondine? This is what we were asking ourselves. Is she the soulless sea-maiden, obsessed with the desire for a soul without being able to weigh up the advantages or disadvantages of actually possessing one? Can she long for love at all, without being able to understand it? What is it that drives her to mix with people? Is she motivated by curiosity, playfulness or the desire for humanity? We came back to these questions again and again. Their answers would be crucial in deciding whether our Huldbrand would be a dreamer who is haunted by visions of Ondine, or a victim of romantic hallucinations, a fickle knight from the Middle Ages, a troubadour, a psychopath, or even just the typical fairytale ballet prince.

Connected to this was the question of the nature of Bertalda, Huldbrand's earthly sweetheart, the sea-maiden's earthly counterpart. Was she merely a haughty maiden from a German *Schloss*, or would it be possible to put her in a more interesting and significant role opposing the nymph? Why does Huldbrand reject Ondine for her?

How far would we be able to avoid reaching back to the characters of ballet scenarios from the nineteenth century, to defend ourselves from the clichés of ballet theatre and at the same time make use of some of the merits of the old *grand ballet*?

And – still more pressing – how far would we be able to avoid, on the other hand, clichés of the modern performing arts, clichés that were all around us, and that could be so effortlessly and universally used? Vibraphone magic, *ostinato* rhythms, electronic sounds to signify the supernatural, twelve-tone chords, alienation effects on the stage, and the countless tricks of surrealism?

Would *Ondine* be completely transformed under the influence of the Mediterranean summer? Should we fight this transformation, or simply let it happen?

The passing days were occupied by these questions, with trumpet blasts from *La Forza del Destino* providing occasional interruptions. A short sketch from Ashton's exercise book shows that there was still a long way to go before we would reach the final version.

Prologue – Act I as it was

Act II ballroom (where Huldbrand was to meet Bertalda)

Act III Bertalda rushes through forest – arriving at boat – boat-scene-vision (Ondine, who has by now returned to the sea) – *marriage* (with Bertalda). *Finale* (as in Fouqué's book) – *Apothéose* (Ondine under the sea with Huldbrand).

Stylistic questions were discussed and resolved for the first time. The nineteenth century, particularly the former half, was a time of clarity and romantic ideas which had produced a flourish of ballet theatre, the like of which could only later be matched by Diaghilev, with similar perspectives, if different content. The ballet of the mid-nineteenth century at the Royal Theatres of Moscow, Naples and London expressed romantic thoughts in its performances, as it attempted to capture the feeling of the time. *Giselle*, the transformation of Heine's *Willis* by Gauthier, Coralli and the uncompromising music of Adam (which loses all prominence in this context), is a work of art of the highest order: unsentimental, full of horror and – particularly in the second act – true poetry. Its composition allows us an exceptionally clear insight into an intellect that combines the serious and deep with something for which we Germans have the rather disparaging word *Gefälligkeit* (pleasantness), but which is actually greater, namely elegance achieved through mastery and restraint of expression.

The teasing fairies in the third act of *La Belle au Bois Dormant* (to cite a second example), when the Prince tries in vain to capture his vision, have nothing of that ridiculous provincial elfin trickery that we see in later decades, but instead provide an ironic, glassy portrayal of that painful confusion in which lovers are trapped. It became our intention that *Ondine* should also achieve such a level of fine emotion, portrayed in so tender a construct. In order to avoid the bridge to the nineteenth century becoming a mere gesture, new forms would need to be found, a flexibility with neither concealment nor disguise, clear and re-strained in equal measure.

The name Huldbrand, so strongly evocative of a Knight from the Middle Ages, was changed to Palemon, and the Knight's maiden Bertalda became Beatrice. Kühleborn, master of the Mediterranean, was changed to the more fitting Tirrenio. These rechristenings were yet another step towards establishing the story in a new setting, even if Ashton could not yet decide to set the whole work in the South. Just as it was possible for an Englishman to be attracted and seduced by Italy, an Italian could also be bewitched by the English landscape and English culture, as would later happen to Miss de Nobili. But that was still a long way off.

Palemon is in love with a vision: even if Ondine actually existed as a real, tangible nymph (and we will be left in doubt over this; do Palemon's friends and Beatrice – who must be doubting his fickleness – see Ondine?), even if Palemon, sur-

Palemon, costume design, Act I

rounded by tritons and nymphs holds 'his' Ondine in his arms in the depths of the forest (or believes he holds her in his arms) and even after a ghostly wedding ceremony with small fauns officiating, this union seems highly implausible. The sea-maiden lacks a human heart and possesses instead only charm, grace and perhaps qualities impossible to name; she is like music, soaring and ageless. She is as nature itself, having no reason, her thoughts without consequence.

If Palemon is in love with Ondine, he is at the same time in love with art; and this union with a vision or a work of art (an ultimate union only possible in death or madness), this desired oblivion is not granted him. The longed-for transformation does not take place, and again and again he is struck by his human failings, which force him back amongst the rest of humanity. Palemon, who remains up to his last heartbeat under the spell of this often rather ill-defined, unfathomable character, is delivered a death towards which he heads inconsistently and whose redeeming beauty he earns not through his faith, but through his pain.

On the day before Ashton's departure we wrote a short summary of our research. This later became a plan whose details were modified again and again during the coming months, indeed right through to the final rehearsals, and which could be briefly outlined as follows:

Synopsis
Act I
One day Palemon, unhappily in love with the proud Beatrice, meets Ondine. The grace of the nymph causes him to forget Beatrice; he follows Ondine into the depths of the forest, to the sea. Tirrenio, master of the Mediterranean, wants to prevent the disastrous bonding between human and ghost. He commands tritons and nymphs to use all their powers of magic and terror to separate Palemon and Ondine. The ghosts, however, are no match for the steadfastness of the knight

Two minutes before the start of the performance:
Margot Fonteyn, Frederick Ashton and Hans Werner Henze

Pas de deux, Act I

and the honesty and depth of his feelings. Beatrice and her friends set off in pursuit of Palemon. Wounded pride and worry keep her on his trail. However, tritons block the way and scatter the crowd who are hunting Palemon.

Act II

A sailing boat waits for Ondine and Palemon in a small harbour. Beatrice, distraught from shock, finds the lovers there. Ondine and Palemon console her and invite her to board the ship with them. On the high seas Ondine's supernatural powers are revealed. She conjures up wind and waves, her sinister playmates. Palemon watches with great alarm. It is now only too easy for Beatrice to turn him against Ondine. Helpless in her innocence, Ondine must now watch as she loses her lover to her cunning earthly rival. Disappointed and filled with pain, she follows the insistent calls of her playmates. She returns to her element... Tirrenio, enraged by the knight's disloyalty, conjures up a storm. The ship is smashed to pieces. Palemon, Beatrice and the sailors save themselves on a reef.

Act III

Palemon is strongly reminded of Ondine. On the evening before his wedding to Beatrice, Ondine's image appears to him. Only the arrival of the wedding guests finally shakes him from his reverie. – A stranger appears, accompanied by a crowd of masked Neapolitans, who enliven the celebration with their dancing. The dance becomes ever more sinister, and the masks are then dropped, revealing water ghosts, who fly furiously around the room. Tirrenio, the stranger, has let them in. – The guests flee, and Beatrice tries in vain to take the enraptured Palemon with her. He remains, alone. – From the depths of the garden Ondine approaches him, her face stained with tears. As they embrace, Palemon must die.

(This synopsis allows later choreographers to fit their own detailed changes into the overall structure.)

Some weeks later I received the *minutage* from Ashton, a treatment of the plot that had been divided up into scenes, alternating between ensemble dances, solos and variations. Every scene had annotations as to the duration, tempo and metre, and even suggestions or questions as to the choice of orchestration. At first glance I doubted whether I would be able to accept such an impingement on my sphere of work, until I noticed, especially after the first attempts, how much these recommendations spoke of a professionalism and competence, a theatrical instinct that knows exactly how long a situation in a scene, a tempo or a sound can last, and how long one can draw on the physical power of a dancer. A lot was being asked of the soloists: Ondine is on stage almost constantly (although she has a somewhat easier time of it in Act III), and her part must count among the most demanding ballet roles of all time, both physically and spiritually.

That autumn I began the sketches for the composition. I chose the larger type of chamber orchestra, comprising two flutes, an oboe, a cor anglais, a clarinet, a bass clarinet, a bassoon, a contrabassoon, four horns, three trumpets, two trombones, a tuba, timpani, a piano (alternating with a celesta), two harps, some percussion and strings. I tried to reconcile myself to the particular needs of a travelling ballet troupe like the Royal Ballet, which changes its orchestra from town to town; in other words, the music would have to lend itself to being performed after minimal rehearsal time. This was a further technical restriction, but at the same time a challenge.

The two harps are from time to time played in concerto style, almost completely avoiding the typical glissandi and arpeggios, their sound representing the ethereal Ondine and her compatriots. This sound sometimes becomes harder, crossing over to the piano or vanishing off into harmonic tones in the strings and the celesta. Thus the sound of weightlessness could be created, set against the dark-sounding elements of the rest of the orchestra, which represent the earthly Palemon. If the dark and light elements were to meet, it would create strong tensions, pain.

Act III

Prelude & Vision   5´ min –
under water.
Pas-de- Supplication
Bert. & Thel interrupted   2 min
Y entrée & promenade of guests   1 min.
Grand Pas Classique   6½ mins.

    Adagio boys & girls   2   ⎫
      Var girls   1½ ⎬ =
        "   Boys   1½ ⎭
       Coda general fast   1½

Entrée of Kubla Kan
Followed by rush of Neopolitans   ¼
Divertissement consists of 12 boys & 12 girls   ½
+ 3 principal boys & 3 principal girls.
i.e. All boys & all girls   1 min ⎫
    into which enter Soloists
    pas- de - six   1
    Pasde - Trois ⎫   1
    2 boys 1 girl ⎭
    pas -de -Trois ⎫   1
    2 girls one boy ⎭
    12 girls & 12 boys   1   ⎬ 11 mins.
    Var 3 girls   1
    Var 1 boy   1
    Var 2 girls   1
    All six to finish   1
    All 12 boys & 12 girls & ⎫ 2
    all pas -de - six.

Solemn dance interrupted by Ondines
in frenzy – flight of Bertalda all
exit = (pas -de - action   2 mins.
Pas -de - deux. O & U.   3 mins.
Apotheosis   1 min ?
                            ———————
                            32¼ mins
          or better   30 mins.

Tirrenio, the King of the tritons, has his own call signs, which the air-and water-ghosts follow, including those below:

Ondine also has her own melodic interval, which sometimes expand into melodic creations. Palemon too has his own world of sound, which mostly appears in low strings and solo woodwind-ariosi that, true to the properties of these instruments, often 'speak' as in an operatic recitative.

In the clear air of Monte di Dio, the noise of the streets now seems far away. From the rocks of the Acropolis, where today weather-beaten ramparts stand, one can look out onto the Bourbon military academy, now flagged with the Italian *tricolore*, and onto the old British embassy and further down to the Castel dell'Ovo. Here the gentler autumn has arrived after the fiery summer, and early in the morning the light appears that will later sparkle crystal-clear, elevating the contours of the landscape as in a drawing in many shades of grey; a pale morning horizon, later pale red, with balloon-like clouds above, reminiscent of photographs of a pre-World War I manoeuvre. The Pompeii-like red of the nearby houses stands out against the steel-coloured sea. Last lights in Mergellina, the fishing port, cocks crowing in the yards, and in the nearby garden friendly birdsong can be heard.

All this exists in the middle of this century, alive, inhabited. Children are growing up in this world in which ancient history is still very real, where the only changes that take place are unnoticeable, fitting in with the more dominant reality of the

Beatrice, costume design, Act I

landscape and its inhabitants, while the modern world in the form of the technology and architecture of the new industrial suburbs laps around the town like a stormy sea, pushing the old town 'forward'. But here dark Greek eyes throw sirocco glances – glances free from 'primeval fear', as if from a fiery star. The Hellenic way of life and thought set the measure for how people act out their lives.

The work begins with quiet woodwind chords and a sustained unison in the strings.

Structure: a twelve-tone progression (expressed horizontally and vertically), which is to crop up from time to time in the work. Its force comes from occasionally straining and breaking (as, for example in the Act II finale) the melodic and harmonic elements, which are not even indirectly connected to it. Shorter sequences from this progression are also to be used as motifs, without the structural aspect of the score becoming dependent on it. The progression should be just one building block among many. – In the twelfth bar pastoral music begins, which should remind us of an old canzone (Lavandaie del Vomero). *Then the curtain is raised: the short overture has already hinted at the presence of air- and water-ghosts, but now there are only people on the stage: Palemon, Beatrice and their friends. The sound is harder, more robust, the rhythm having something of the* danses générales *of Adam and Délibes. Later, when Palemon is alone, Ondine appears to him: there is an Ondine call, which will carry through the work undergoing many variations,*

Danse générale, Act I

Danse générale, Act I

somewhat reminiscent of the sound of the original chords. At this point for the first time we hear both harps being played, similar to two pianos; their effect does not come from glissandi and harmonies, but through exhibiting the true quality of the harp: that strange, tentative production of sounds. Ondine's shadow dance is an interplay of quick and slow (here the harps also play concerto-style, accompanied by deep solo strings and isolated woodwind), towards the end becoming more agitated, panicked; Palemon's shadow has suddenly fallen on Ondine.

In January I came to London and began an interesting period of work. Every morning I would work on the music, discussing its feasibility with Ashton in the afternoon. The old piano in the small studio in Yeoman's Row trembled at the triton music's hard blows; the floor and furniture became covered with notepaper; there were discussions, points of controversy, new plans, changes for the fifth and sixth time. Slowly we began to reach agreement, after doing battle with each other, testing the ground and then finally taking account of each other's point of view.

1. Ashton's problems and vexing questions: would this new Continental composer be able to do justice to our ideas? Would he be able to write a ballet that will not immediately scare off the 3,000-strong Covent Garden audience? What can I do to fit his music to the project, and to what extent can I force him to renounce the uncompromising hardness of his style for the sake of what I would like to achieve? How can I explain his music to my dancers, even if it is simpler than his concert music? What does he actually take the word 'melody' to mean?

2. Henze's problems and vexing questions: How can I live up to the task that I have been set without compromising on the technical standards of 'new music'? To what extent will a theatre audience be ready and willing to follow a difficult contrapuntal device? Is it even worthwhile to introduce complicated elements into ballet music, which will neither be heard, nor contribute to the clarity or compre-

hensibility of the action on stage? Should I not completely sacrifice my emotions for the sake of providing opportunities for the great ballerinas to jump, run, turn and express themselves on stage? Will I be able to convince Ashton of the new, unusual but perfectly usable 'cantability' of my compositions?

Thus it was that our work could only progress slowly, the picture only gradually becoming clearer. Research was started; attempts to push back the frontiers of 'danceability', attempts to achieve a light homophony, which is what the work demanded. Evening after evening was spent at ballet performances, studying the relationship between dance and music, those inexplicable, uncharted moments of happy concord... observing the art of Margot Fonteyn, studying her melodiousness, attempting to comprehend the highest moments of her adagios. A feeling of restlessness, the joy of being useful for something, when we all, painter, choreographer, dancers, work together to create something new, entering into a communication whose results cannot be predicted, like an exciting journey.

Every new work of art is the sum of those that have gone before it. In finishing it, the author feels more complete, only to discover with the passing of time that this work was just a transition, an instant of time held still, whose main value to the author lies in providing hope and courage for another experience. The next work goes against the previous one in that it shatters what were its most perfect moments. The more perfectly and powerfully this process of eradication occurs, the more easily the new and unknown opens up to the author. As a consequence it becomes possible to withdraw ever further from being comparable to contemporaries.

Infinitives: To allow the listener an unmathematically exact experience (only the unmathematical can be exact); to try to allow excitement to be expressed in the music – elements and developments that can be

Sketch of the wedding scene, Act II

valued by no means other than the purely intuitive art of intervals. To recognise that the music will always make use of the wrong gesture here and there: formulae are no longer important. Original painful experience has become mere convention; the motions have remained, but the life-blood has ebbed away. To stop using the all too familiar methods of modern composition; to trust one's ear more than recognised conventions. To abandon normal meeting places, to prepare to listen to new voices, who do not simply chime in with a new 'direction', but who carry a message, like foreign birds of passage from unknown lands. To be ready at any moment to sacrifice anything for a new stimulus, a new experience, a new world. To postpone ultimate decisions as long as possible, to be ever prepared for new solutions, rapid changes of direction.

Tirrenio enters the stage with wild leaps. Alexander Grant's Tirrenio had been experimenting with the rhythm of this dance for some time in London. Pure madness, to treat difficult rhythmic sequences as dance music. They dominate the dancing and rob the choreographer of the freedom to invent creative movement sequences. As so often in this ballet, it turned out that a regular beat was appropriate, as the motions of the choreography form a much more convincing counterpoint to it: quick passages in the music are set off by slow action on the stage, and vice versa.

The contrast of music and action can be used to great dramatic effect. For the *maratona di danza* (Berlin 1957) I remember the choreographer Dick Sanders (with Jean Babilée and Marion Zito) experimenting with setting a *pas de deux* to Schubert's *Impromptu in B minor*. The resulting smooth movements were fascinating, and during the rehearsals we stared eagerly at the duo on stage. After some time Sanders took the music away and replaced the recorded music, which had initially been use=d for this scene, by jazz. The effect of the two side-by-side was overwhelming. The whole of the ballet *Le Jeune Homme et la Mort* (Cocteau, Roland Petit) was produced in a similar way – that brilliant *pas d'action* between Babilée and Nathalie Philipart. The rehearsals were done to jazz music, mainly in fact to animate the almost improvised movements of both dancers. Then, for the dress rehearsal, the jazz music was removed and the orchestra played Bach's *Passacaglia in C minor*. Babilée synchronised the action solely with the music's duration (not with its features) by occasionally looking at his watch…

At this point Grant, in London, made himself spokesman for the group's wishes in terms of music. I tried to take account of these feelings and wishes in my considerations, and our conver-

Beatrice and the fishermen, Act II

sations often provided valuable food for thought. We once went
on a walk that began under the arches of Whitehall. I tried to
explain my new melodic technique to Grant, and managed by
singing (at any rate better than by playing the piano) to convince
him of a line like the one in the shadow dance.

The singing went on until we reached the Thames (where,
on the other side, the lights were going on in the Houses of
Parliament). We walked along the river under the bare maple
trees. At one point a golden second-empire eagle rose over the
trees, so close as to appear unnatural, ending its flight in the
Trafalgar Square area. (There, thousands of starlings were rushing
through the air like a wind. They gathered there every evening, I
was told. They have an agitated, almost cruel squawk, the breath
of the North. Everywhere one is reminded – not merely by the
presence of the Thames – that the city is near the sea.)

*Tirrenio comes onto the stage with wild leaps, underscored by ener-
getic impulses from the orchestra. Tirrenio calls his ghosts. Accompanied
by an even-tempered quaver motif, which starts in the cellos and low
woodwind before ascending through to the highest instruments, Tirrenio's
first call is sounded in the lowest brass, ending in the high trumpets like
an alarm call. A secondary theme (a scherzo for the woodwind) leads
back to the dark, even quavers of the opening, to which the cor anglais*

*plays a melody for the first time, the fragment of a tune that will keep
appearing between Palemon and Ondine.*

*Fouqué: 'If you are not really there, merely flitting airily around me,
then I do not want to live in the real world either, and will become a
shadow like you, dear, dear Ondine.' This is expressed in the violin
melody. We see the lovesick Palemon crossing the forest. Lively demi-
semiquavers in the harps and staccato semiquavers in the woodwind, set
above chords in the horns and trombones and short-lived signal-calls in
the flutes and oboes, announce the arrival of tritons and nymphs who are
now hurrying to keep Palemon from Ondine, and to put him to the test.
The tempo of the music becomes more lively, its character more accented
as it darts and strains. The more Palemon worries and fights for his
vision, the more we hear variations, raising the excitement from one
eight-bar sequence to the next. The previous theme 'Palemon speaks to
Ondine' is overlaid to an ever greater extent with other voices, calls on
the horn, glissandi, trills, syncopations, a rolling battery of small drums
and tambourines, and then everything changes to a* tutti *of frantic
strings, with high trumpets. This is followed by a new sequence of
variations, beginning with a new rhythm that soon fills the whole
orchestra. Towards the end it is in danger of getting carried away with
itself, but then the deep, even quavers reappear, over which Palemon's
song builds up like a pyramid, until it stands immaculate in clear,
peaceful chords in the brass. Palemon's steadfastness has won the day,
and he holds Ondine in his arms.*

Reports about *Ondine*: in 1844 the ballet *Ondine* was staged by Jules Perrot in the Drury Lane Theatre. The *Morning Herald* wrote of the choreographer:

'Perrot possesses a delicate feeling for beauty and his compositions seem to have been created with a classical sensibility, which, were it to be directed towards another art form, would merit admiration at an altogether higher level. His configurations are worthy of recording for posterity. What a shame that they are so fleeting. They come like shadows and disappear the same way.'

Ashton has an oil painting showing the ballerina Fanny Cerrito performing the *arabesque* of her shadow dance in Perrot's *Ondine*. Another Ondine was Miss Frampton, who burnt to death horrifically when her tutu caught fire on a gas lamp on the stage of the Drury Lane Theatre during a performance. Once again, the legendary, fascinating tension between fire and water.

Also during a performance of *Ondine* in 1844, the dancer Plunkett pushed her colleague Miss Scheffer against a backdrop in a fit of jealousy. The unlucky dancer stumbled and tore a cord from which a lamp was hanging, thereby extinguishing the light for the moon in the scenery, to much noise and protest from the audience. Perrot appeared in front of the curtain and calmed the audience with the words: '*Mesdames et messieurs, un accident impossible à prevoir a dérangé la machine de la lune ... c'est une éclipse complète.*'

The finale begins with dark calls on the horns, which are taken up in modified form by muted trumpets. Beatrice and friends hurry into the forest to recover Palemon. The tempo changes suddenly; a vivace *in 3/4 time starts; one of Beatrice's party is torn to pieces, the whole orchestra becoming extremely animated as the ghosts chase and dispel the human invaders. Chromatic notes run through the woodwind, from the lowest to the very highest instruments, and on which a panicked excitement breaks out repeatedly. The crescendo is followed by a short, calm phase (mime: Beatrice meets the hermit who shows her the way to the sea), and from here we progress to the final passage, a triumphant dance by the ghosts who follow Beatrice as she breathlessly flees. Short motifs, too wild to form a galliard, but distantly resembling one in their rhythm, are accompanied by continuous triplets, crossing between strings and brass. It becomes even more tumultuous than before, the syncopated beats of the galliard-like motifs becoming more compact, harder and eventually pushing forward to the final chord, a wild cry from Tirrenio.*

Once the music for the first act had been written, I played it to Ashton, and whenever my inadequate piano playing allowed him to concentrate on the music, he noted the points where, despite previous warnings, I had overrun the timings set down in the *minutage*. Here and there it was possible to weed out these mistakes by abridging or removing passages, but in the *danse générale* described above – which had become in total about one-and-a-half minutes longer than planned – I refused to change anything, and consequently it went into production in this 'overlong' state. Even a quarter of a minute is a long time in the theatre, especially in ballets. The dance steps available for a particular moment are quickly exhausted and something that has been clearly stated once can then only be repeated, a process that lends no further impact. That is the reason for the *minutage*, providing the advantage of a well-worked-out overview of how time is divided between accents and main themes. From this point on I redoubled my efforts to keep to the tempos on which we had agreed, and tried to see each bar of the music purely as a theatrical element, in order to avoid any deviation.

Ashton had rediscovered many theatrical practices that had been often neglected, even forgotten – many things which by that time were deemed old-fashioned or outmoded. In this I learnt a lot from him, as I have done again and again from Luchino Visconti, whose culture and profound knowledge of

Italian theatre's past inspire and propel me towards new forms.

That form of theatre from the Bauhaus era which one so often encounters these days – vaguely described as 'modern' and putting Bauhaus experimentation into practice – forces one to think up new ideas, since its practices have become all to easy to imitate. Ideas like that of 'interior design', 'room design' and 'room form' have now moved into the public domain, and can these days be seen in the décor of espresso bars, cinemas and station restaurants; the 'expressive fragmentism' of the set designer, who cut through the stage with a 'radical liberation from decoration', had been completed by the previous generation with all the consequences that it duly incurred. And today one may dare to ask whether it is not already time to demand something of the stage, which in its virtuosity and responsibility goes a level beyond those solutions that have already become comfortable routine. And whether – in a way that is appropriate for us, but just as intensively as back then at the birth of 'abstract theatre' – we should see the production of theatrical art as an artistic and social effort: an effort that demands the avoidance of every routine, demanding instead all the sensitivity and freedom that we possess in this era of debasement, of reduction, of the levelling of people's tastes.

The form that has proven itself to work is not enough. Music is more than a discipline. New insights and works are exposed to a criticism whose value system does not apply to them, as even the most advanced criticism stops short at an aesthetic formed decades ago. Even this most advanced criticism would fail to understand the behaviour of the new work; it will not fit into any box, even the boxes that have just been made, and it takes it upon itself always to be where one least expects it. It has no registration number around its neck; it is like an air- or water-ghost, incomprehensible, impossible to grasp, puzzling, above all when rational analysis believes that it has the measure of it.

Pas de trois, Act II

We live in an era where a falsely formed sense of identity has become widespread, a pseudoidentity; but the feeling of being elevated in modernity provides no escape. One can only be on the trail of a time; it is not possible to enter into the consciousness of a time in order to represent it. One can express oneself in a time, as suffering that time. Great artists like Michelangelo and Mozart left a mark on their time, but it was the protest against their time that gave them breath, and allowed them to stay true to life. The 'moment of truth' – that life-or-death moment between bull and matador – is, one must suppose, to be found in an emotional no-man's-land, where occasionally a light flashes if one keeps one's eyes open. This is perhaps where the decision is made, a decision that must be taken completely alone, one whose validity will be measured solely on its creative merits under critical scrutiny and by way of its sensibility. The 'moment of truth' is not to be found in the adoption of ready-made, fashionable devices, nor in paraphrasing them.

The curtain rises as the first chord is played, a chord from the climax of the Act I danse générale. A tenor bassoon, accompanied by pizzicati and other woodwind interjections, cites the canzone Sceta Te, a fishing song; the strings take it further, while low harps, trombones and timpani play an even-tempered quaver movement. This is often to return during the act (and once more in Act III), representing the light rocking of the ship, which is just being rigged up at this point. Small percussion instruments herald a new section, a little duo for two flutes, to which the rocking, the percussion music and the canzone are added, so that four strands of music are present at the same time. All of these are attempts to capture in the sound something of the morning melancholy of a harbour such as Torre del Greco, with its seclusion and muteness which can be read from old engravings and which still exists in real life today. This montage-like, four-headed creation flows into an adagio for high strings, a variation on the climax of the danse générale, in pianissimo (Palemon's love triumphant).

Theatre people often recommend that musical themes (sounds, themes, motifs, rhythms) be repeated (giving, as they do, such clarity and reinforcement); but this unchanged reintroduction of a theme into the action on stage has something solid and mechanical about it, while it seems to me that theatre music should show in a poetic manner how time dramatically glides by – that there is no return. Perhaps this teaches us something of an era in which the *leitmotif* had not yet been invented. It will never again be 2pm on this March afternoon. A piece of music, even when we hear it on the same record, under the same external conditions as yesterday, is different from how it was yesterday, or different from how we heard it yesterday. Unpredictable as our imagination is when applied to our listening and writing, we know at least that it does not return to things that we have discovered; they no longer occupy us once we have captured them on paper.

From this it must follow that if the principles of returning themes mentioned above are to serve drama, they can be justified only if they are used in a quite poetic spirit – forced to return, their previous sense changed, as an inversion or variation, representing the changes and developments in the human activity of the story. In this way the music can be kept far away from enslavement by the leitmotif, and also from the non-committal nature of so-called 'concert theatre'. The music would be in a dimension in which it has sovereignty, setting the tone, providing the reason for the exaltation that drives those on stage to sing and dance. If we accept that realism and truth in non-religious theatre are possible, then its music can be seen as a real being, with movable limbs like a living organism, ready to rise and fall, to be a part of life, to illuminate it as only it can (to say what cannot be said), and once again to dare to encounter the human voice and the human body – those bearers of truths, so limited, so hard to reach. Perhaps musical theatre could lose all of its artificial, nebulous qualities and achieve an actuality based on new, free music that is no longer hermetically isolated.

Following on from the adagio, *which is a variation of the 'If you are not really there, merely flitting airily around me', is the* pas des mate-lots, *an animated figure in the violins with a countermelody in the woodwind and brass. The 2/2 rocking from before provides a counterpoint in the bass. The violins run into no. III; the departure of the sailing ship begins. Trills working up to a crescendo herald a wavering brass phrase, to which the ship's sails billow as the land and the harbour vanish from view. The boat is on the high seas. We hear again the rocking quavers in the deep sections of the orchestra, overlaid with a dialogue between violins and a guitar.*

This very calm passage is followed by a piece that Ashton named 'rocking dance'; the rocking moves from two quavers to triplets and the music becomes more animated, swelling, quickening still further, then rushing and animated, only then to fall back to the original rocking. (Ondine, playing with the elements, working them into a frenzy, only to calm them again, filled with consternation at the distress she has caused to the ship's crew.)

The pas de trois *begins here. Instead of following the Ondine–Palemon–Beatrice conflict portrayed in this dance in a late-romantic leitmotif style, the music here has the function of a spotlight, to a certain extent shining down on the action from above. This can also perhaps be interpreted as the invisible ghosts voicing their unhappiness about Ondine. The music is aria-like but without the dramatic accents (one might cautiously describe it as baroque-Neapolitan). The reprise of the first theme in the* pas de trois *is interrupted by a clarinet recitative (Beatrice has snatched away the amulet from Palemon), which is then continued by a solo viola and then a solo violin. A short variation follows (a variation in the musical as well as the ballet sense of the word) for Beatrice, who is playing with the amulet.*

Lila de Nobili came from Paris to London, as it was time to talk about the scenery and the costumes. She listened to the

Costume design for the *grand pas*

music to Act I, performed by Robert Irving, Musical Director of the Royal Ballet, and to fragments of Act II. Judging from the words written on the notepad about this first meeting of choreographer, composer and set designer, we can imagine how difficult it was for three authors from quite different cultures to find common ground, to complement each other and to reach agreeable solutions. In such cases it is the music that is the deciding factor, but even here there were difficulties: very few people possess the ability to imagine from the sober tones of the piano score how the full orchestra will later sound. (This even eludes musicians for the most part.) In addition, each person hears music in a unique way – it may evoke colourful, animated images in one person that are completely different from the responses of the next.

What is needed here, therefore, is to inform the choreographer and set designer of the expected sound of the orchestra with as few technical terms and as many everyday words as possible. Despite these precautionary measures, and especially when dealing with unknown music with an as yet unimaginable sound, misunderstandings arise, often with serious, critical effects on the success of the production. For this reason a successful communication between dance, décor and music can be spoken of as a real stroke of luck. Clashes between the colour on the stage and the colour of the instrumental sound, or conceptual mistakes in the choreography, even if they appear minor or disturb the harmony only briefly, all produce a feeling of unease, which even a less well-educated audience picks up on. The musician must struggle to be understood again and again, beginning with his closest friends and ending with his enemies. This need for expression engulfs first the hopeful members of the company, then spreads out over the massed, anonymous, sceptical dark ranks of the audience of the opening night, and ends with needling and body-blows from the far distance, from where the snakes and dragons peep out of their hiding holes.

From the words written in the notebook we can see that Lila de Nobili suggested that the ballet's set design should follow the old Italian technique, and furthermore that a reconstruction of the ballet style of La Scala from the first half of the nineteenth century should be attempted. Her knowledge of history and of the old theatrical style, which she seemed to be in love with, fuelled her imagination, and we latched on to her first suggestions with interest. Ashton loves the Gothic revival (Fonthill Abbey etc.), although I do not share his view, and he was unwilling not to have elements of this style in the ballet's décor. Another subject of discussion was the Regency style, as the fashion of this period also had a variant with a light Neapolitan influence. This was thrown into question when the music was heard. The music allows the choreographer and set designer to conjure up the nineteenth century and its style of ballet, but the difficulty lies in the fact that such an evocation of a previous time must not be confused with a simple reconstruction, but must instead be made visible by mutating it: just as in the case of the music, where references to the past — motifs from the old ballet music — appear as nostalgic shadows. In this one has to entrust oneself to the alertness and sensitivity of one's colleagues.

At that point it was not possible to get a final answer from Lila de Nobili to questions about the scenic realisation of the work. She wanted first to make sketches of it, and then to decide whether she could begin. The early *ottocento* seemed plausible as a stylistic stimulus, since, as has already been said, the music was inspired from that time, from the thoughts of young men such as Heine and Fouqué, who saw the sylphs flying through the forest. But we could not allow ourselves to fall back into the feeling of this time; it might be a stimulus, an inspiration, a starting point, but not a sanctuary. On the other hand it would not be possible for our forest to have anything of the forests of Max Ernst, nor anything of the sorcery of Paul Klee, nor the dark, playful horrors of Miro. A new state of suspense would have to be created, a *balance à trois* between today's consciousness, our own desire for expression and that faraway landscape.

Famous ballet decoration from the most recent past – such as Cocteau's *L'Amour et son Amour*, the cool sky full of stars above Jean Babilée's *entrechats*, or the fiery style of Clavé for Roland Petit's *Carmen* – are today, even after only ten years, signs of a beauty that now belongs irretrievably to the past and is no longer applicable to us. While such treasures are still 'used' in poor copies, which try in vain to tarnish their already timeless shine, our expectations had once again turned to new designs and new, original perspectives.

Many things that up to that point had remained unclear to us found an answer for the first time in our conversations with Lila. In the forest of Act I, with its waterfalls and faun faces, we could imagine something like the castle gardens of Caserta, those dramatically inspired allegories on the threshold between baroque and classicism, bathed in fountain spray, surrounded by single trees, so precious in this barren landscape; above it the rocks and boulders of a treeless mountain range, below the clear expanse of the sea.

It was by thinking of Caserta that it became possible to give the forest a location close to the Mediterranean harbour (in the choreography one can pick out here and there something of the characteristics of a group of statues such as Acteon and Diana, with their cool vehemence). From there the way to the Act III interior was not difficult. Whenever we tried to combine English with Italian, hot with cold, light with dark, nighttime and daytime scenes, it occurred to us how many spiritual and romantic connections there were between England and the Kingdom of the two Sicilies: Caserta has an English garden, Lady Hamilton lived in the Villa Roseberry in Posillipo, and Byron, Keats and Shelley were inspired by the landscape and way of life of this cutthroat, gallant land of the South, which to them was a paradise.

A memory of a young street trader in Naples: he had cherries for sale, and his beautiful voice carried the ancient song of his trade with great cheer out over the Via S. Biagio dei Librai. The intervals of his song would later form the basis of Tirrenio's second cry, which is heard as he appears for the first time in Act II during the swelling of the rocking dance, and also when he later calls up the storm in which disloyal Palemon's ship is destroyed.

The man was wearing a crown made out of cherry-tree twigs, leaves and fruit, and this decoration made him appear as majestic as a king, distant, with a special dignity and his ancient song. He was also remarkably similar to the fauns used in theatre decoration at the end of the seventeenth century. Thus the sound and appearance of our Tirrenio were influenced by an unknown King of the Cherries.

How far would the transformative powers of the painter's imagination be able to elevate the work from our original reflections, giving the necessary expression to our wishes, efforts and ideas? The answer came in the form of small, meticulous sketches, which could soon be viewed in the de Nobilis Studio in Paris, Rue de Lille 9, sprayed exactitudes in dark tones on a base of autumnal brown and ochre, glistening gold, the white allowing the sporadic highlights of blue and red to come through only hesitantly and in matte shades.

Here the first departures could be seen, forerunners of the breaks with what is traditional, known, available. These had to form in the painter's imagination before there could be a clearer interpretation of the music, which itself had to interpret both the dance and the painting. Nymphs

Palemon and Beatrice, Act III

*with eyes of honey under wild, long hair, which seemed to be dripping
with water; hunters in hectic, romantic poses; illuminated waterfalls at
night; and an elegant, imaginary ship in bright light – all in a very small
format, meticulous gouaches, from which it was almost impossible to
imagine how they could fill a stage. While Ashton was fired up with the
heat and light of Mediterranean lands, and figures from Greek mythol-
ogy and Neapolitan* pulcinellas *and* tarantellas *flowed into his muse,
the lady from Florence was becoming ever more taken by the English
theatre, pushing her original Mediterranean concept deeper into the
shadows of the 'Gothic revival'. So it was that once again the remarkable
tension between hot and cold, between light and dark arose: in his
'Abbey' under the English moon, the English aesthete of 1803 dreamt
up his Naples, an unreal fairytale city whose contours were blurred; a
playground for sea maidens.*

*Lila de Nobili painted the backdrops alone. Supported by one assist-
ant, Jean-Marie Simon, she spent long weeks in a shed that the theatre
rented for her, so that she could repeat the extraordinarily painstaking
detail in the full-size version. This seems to be the only way that
'enlargement' is possible for her. The pure qualities of painting contained
in each backdrop would be reduced by another's hand. Reflections of
light, water effects, temperatures, all would come alive in these mono-
logues, which scarcely needed the help of a modern stage-lighting system
to produce their effect.*

*A similar work process, which seemed at first glance rather over the
top, was underway for the costumes. Old fabrics from Prato, from the
Marché aux Puces in Paris and London's Portobello Road formed the
basis, while old jewellery, sequins, strings of beads, moss and animal hair
made up the foundation of the imaginative and unusual presentation of
the air- and water-ghosts. Japanese silk and artificial hair, curled in the
old-fashioned way, turned the tender girls of the* corps de ballet *into
beautiful but terrifying spirits of the elements. All through this process
the principle of the rather grandiose, operatic style of La Scala was
retained, rendered fresh and contemporary by the method's unexpected*

reprise, set so completely at odds with the bleak, pared-down style of recent decades. A shock effect, confusing, almost offensive, borne by an authentic, imaginative reality. Here and there 'taken too far', as so often happens with new productions.

The majority of ballet enthusiasts have only just become accustomed to the leotards and black curtains of the Balanchine style, and yet for them it is already becoming synonymous with 'contemporary' and 'modern', while younger elements are planning a new theatrical coup, throwing the current standards into question.

Do not trust the abstract movement in painting… question its usability in theatre… recognise in theatre – which forms the most immediate meeting place for artist and audience – the apex of artistic expression… Entrust to theatre an artistic, not polemic, activity, which goes beyond that of the more intimate studio concert or private gallery… Be wary of the collective term 'modern art'…

Meanwhile Ashton showed the first scenes that he had produced with Margot Fonteyn and Michael Somes: Palemon's meditation in Act I, Ondine's first appearance, her shadow dance, her flight. It was unforgettable: the famous ballet studio in Baron's Court, the great ballerina, her partner, both of them present in duplicate in the long mirrors above the bars, the high windows framing the black London sky. The music from the out-of-tune piano echoed in the empty studio, music conceived with much difficulty, whose past would now be carried away by those so fleet of foot. The delusion and sorrow of the story came alive, the elements began to enliven one another, to heighten each other, sounds captured in diagonals – a new beauty seemed to be born, one that seemed to want to be stronger and more enduring than the preceding worldly factors that gave rise to it.

Ashton had found points of contact with the music that led to the core of the work.

Ashton was surely able to draw on the experience gained from more

Shadow dance, Act I

Mime, Act II

than fifty works of ballet. The basis was his personal neoclassical style, developed through thirty years of work, inspired by the first meetings with Ida Rubinstein and Massine and into which modern practices were also able to flow freely – even those of the 'free dance' (Joos, New German Dance) without pointed toe, which he usually regarded with scepticism. After numerous shorter works of one scene, one motif, the reconstruction of Prokofiev's Romeo and Juliet *for the Royal Danish Ballet, after* Daphnis and Chloe *and* Sylvia, Ondine *was to be the first full-length work to carry itself entirely alone. The ensembles of the* corps de ballet *were already pre-formed in a work like* Dante Sonata *(1939) and in scenes such as* Fire *in* Homage to the Queen *(1952). The starting points for the lyrical scenes stem from the same ballet, and in particular* Water *and* Fire *from* Homage *make the transition to the new ballet, enraptured meditations from which all outward signs have been removed and whose nobility lies in the fact that all effects of common bravura have been eliminated.*

New ways of working with the music: in a break with the antiquated practice seen in the nineteenth century, often still used today and mistakenly held to make musical sense, the dancers' steps are not in time with the music - except for a few isolated moments, for dramatic reasons. What could be simpler than repeating a musical score in all its detail in dance, and what could be more obvious? Instead, Ashton lets the dance behave autonomously; he sets his own counterpoints and balances to the music. At no point in the Act I danse générale *is a rhythmic element from the music reproduced choreographically. Instead there is an independence of form, which allows both music and dance not to submit to one another but instead to fit, carry, complement each other. In order to achieve this, the choreographer had to commit to an extraordinarily in-depth study of the score, the first stage of which consisted of the usual transcription of musical notes to dance moves. But it didn't stop there: here is where the real work began, where a relationship towards the music was developed, where the symbols on the page began to be transformed.*

The crowning glory of the creation, the gleaming centre of

the entire choreographic work, was Margot, the *assoluta*, the fragile instrument, the master's Stradivarius. It was from her that the most beautiful, tender, touching movements came. Her influence can be seen in her nymph sisters, and even the sharp contrasts in the movements of her earthly counterparts seem ultimately to flow from her, seeming to gain an intensity which one can only explain as their astonishment at this hovering miracle, who seems scarcely to touch the ground. From her first appearance, Margot is the fragile vessel of Ashton's poetry. A movement of her body, a glance, *a port de bras*, her hovering movement to a cantilena, and the portrait of the wondrous Ondine is complete. Later there are changes, moments of terror and confusion, which are relieved by expressions of childlike innocence, uncanny and elfin, a scent of mortality, of death.

Who is Ondine? The great *assoluta* has provided a trembling, pulsating answer. She has found herself in Ondine, whose first view of the human world is filled with the gentle pain of anticipation and whose charming exterior scarcely conceals her readiness for disappointment and loneliness. Even love's secret seems to be hidden in her eerie, quiet calls, her enraptured, unattainable nature…

… and it is also because the rules have been broken, with changes to vocabulary no longer following tradition. The sense of being moved and upset are too strong to permit only what is technical, objective. *Elle fait pleurer.*

The transition from mime to pure dance is almost unnoticeable in this choreography; the boundaries become blurred so that it is scarcely possible to tell one from the other, or to know how to define them. Ashton tells his stories with nonchalance; absorbed with the creation of dance, he leaves the plot to fend for itself, so that one sometimes thinks that it has been abandoned, suspended, until the start of a new scene reminds us of the story for a moment.

He answers a rhythm in the orchestra with his own counter-rhythm

Masks, Act III

in dance. Wonderful pirouettes seem to emerge from a sustained chord. A sudden fortissimo *throws the dancers into the air and causes a rush of jumps and whirls that seem to be an echo of the previous instrumental effect, while the music, once again left to itself, can continue. The two elements, having been separated, suddenly rush back towards one another to affect each other again. The choreographer spans a phrase with a long diagonal, counterpoints steady music with* allegro, *or he finds that a heavy slowness works as a dramatic* ritardando *to a flighty passage. Then there are moments where everyone stands still, with their ear inclined to the orchestra, listening, a moment of controlled silence, as if the music coursed straight through their bodies.*

The panicky impression of the omnipresence of water and storms in the air — of waterfalls, of the indomitable force of the sea — is created quite without the help of lighting effects or projections. In fact the opposite is the case: it is achieved by perfectly 'normal' production methods such as painting and dance. Human dwellings, human landscapes are pervaded by the supernatural presence of the ghosts. Even in Act II, where the dance is reduced to a minimum, and where decoration and show seem to take priority true to the old ballet style, no modern theatrical effects are called upon for help. The few there are come from the old practices of La Scala — and even here the ballerina is triumphant, overpowering Palemon's melancholy recitation, overcoming three or four sudden apparitions of fearful, beautiful Tirrenio.

Throughout the three acts, Ashton's inimitable, unconventional hand can be seen: the expression of his culture, his life, his spirit, from whose closed and silent nature the dreamy inventions of movable sculpture spring forth like something absolutely essential, chaste, controlled.

What is Ondine? How is it possible for a person in a modern city (where behind the new glass palaces the rubble from the catastrophe still lies), with a modern brain, whose rational thoughts are normally filled with petrol tanks and electrical equipment, to suddenly remember old fairy tales? But is Ondine simply a fairy-tale figure, does she remove us from reality, taking us away from our time? Or does she really exist in a timeless state as a spirit, a feeling of weightlessness, a remnant of tenderness that has survived and whose recognition as but a small cause will have unexpectedly significant effects? Just as in her fairy-tale world, where the contrast between hot and cold provokes tensions – the separation of land and water, of the physical and the spiritual – her presence in a modern-day consciousness is the trigger for tensions between hardness and tenderness, steel and silk, rawness and sensitivity, the city's mass pathos and lonely forlornness. Temptation and will-o'-the-wisp in one, her being has something of a crystal's clarity, in which centuries reflect and merge.

The active rediscovery of values from an earlier culture and the act of writing down such discoveries in notes, texts, pictures and dance steps can only superficially be called 'romanticism'. An artistic behaviour such as this, which calls upon the old for help in its path to renewal, in part out of a feeling of historical continuity, in part for purely aesthetic reasons such as the need for clarity, often seems less easy to understand or easier to misinterpret in its results than a direct adoption of the practices of the time. The further the range of expressive possibilities extends both upwards and downwards, the more the core seems out of reach and the more difficult it seems for the observer to define what the artist was trying to achieve. Perhaps this is because the observer is too close, or perhaps the field of vision is too small, perhaps because the sudden and unannounced changes to the movement cannot be understood when one tries to use criteria on them that really should only be used on a sort of art exercise or art interpretation.

'People living in a world of darkness desperately need your help.'
(Inscription in the passenger compartment of London taxis.)

The Royal Opera House lies in the heart of London's answer to Les Halles, the large vegetable market of Covent Garden, adjacent to the much more impressive Victorian market hall. Walking to the theatre in the morning, one enters (slipping on a cabbage leaf or the remains of some fruit) into the dense traffic of vans and carts loaded with fruit and vegetables, fresh from the provinces. In the *Nag's Head* pub opposite the opera house, children of the muse commune in brotherly fashion with the cheerful porters, deliverymen and wholesalers of the market for a morning drink. It is hardly pleasant here, but it does have a certain quality, something of the world of Dickens and its magic. The light is almost always murky, the humid mist taking us on a rainy journey from dawn to dusk.

Perhaps because of all the smoke and greyness, the opera house has become very much the place where Londoners can encounter things of beauty. Margot Fonteyn seems to have become the stuff of legend for the aficionados of the many ballet clubs up and down the land. After each of her performances the narrow street that runs down the side of the opera house is completely blocked by young people wanting to see the dancer; with a great deal of effort police officers form a gangway for the few steps from the stage door to the taxi which awaits the tender, pale lady with the enormous eyes, to take her, swan queen, firebird, aurora, away into the mist.

… The Londoners seem to have found a rareness in the beauty that this dancer embodies. They take great pride in the beautiful, loving it like a cherished possession, and artists, pioneers on expeditions to wondrous lands, are held in high regard.

Art is always in danger and must be constantly reinvented in order to fend off the invasion of the mechanical, the constant march of monotony and cement.

Masks, Act III

Winter days with a little sun, which at least in the morning is visible through the haze, turning the air pink and causing an animated glistening on the river, like a Turner painting. On the sandbanks not far from the docks, the white swans, property of the Crown, are resting, and others glide majestically on the dark waters: highlights, counterpoints, letting the heavy barges pass — no acknowledging glance is exchanged, no courtesy. One thinks back to the dancers in the opera house, to Tchaikovsky, to

Swanilda and Odile, the black swan. The fairy tale continues in
real life, and reality seems more real and at the same time more
fantastic than the evening life of the ballerinas beyond the orchestra. Their seclusion, their precise song continues throughout
the day on the great river, secretive yet visible to everyone. And
death is as close to them in the day as in the evening – the
hunter's arrow hits the beautiful swans in the beam of the flood-
lights. The pain that such a fall from heaven brings is repeated
when we learn that hundreds of these royal birds have perished
in the last few days, suffocating in the oil of a sunken tanker.

Battersea amusement park lies on the bank of the river, a
permanent institution dating from the Festival of Britain, in
which a few workers can be seen in the spring, busy applying a
fresh coat of paint to strange, seemingly unusable carousels, futile
dreamboats and grotesque flying machines. These things were
constructed by London painters and sculptors such as Suther-
land, Moore, Piper and others, for the users of the amusement
park, mostly workers and their children.

Downstream from Battersea Bridge are the Battersea paper
mills. Anonymous letters, bills and bad reviews are collected here.
Heavily laden boats gently travel down the Thames to the sea,
where the paper is thrown overboard, food for the insatiable
herrings and flounders.

When attending a concert in the Festival Hall, one is reminded of the incredible closeness of the river upon which the
concert hall stands, similar to Covent Garden, a place of beauty
in the middle of docks and factories. The enormous organ pipes
of the great hall seem to be inspired by the life of the river: they
recall the chimneys on the boats, or perhaps pipes through
which the black water flows. And the sound they produce can
perhaps also not unreasonably be compared to the foghorns that
call out with longing from the more distant steamers, with a
minor fifth, a triton.

Perhaps in such pictures we find an explanation for the superficially cast judgement that whenever something unknown or foreign precludes the possibility of some other terminology being used, it is currently stamped with the term 'romanticism'. But the present-day world around us is filled with beautiful new words, pictures and sounds, precious precisely because they have grown up and continue to grow in all their vulnerability among the grey, deadening surroundings of our time. New insights into the reality of a young art form that actively looks into life and wants to interact with it can therefore by no means be summed up using a terminology coined for something from the past. The misused word 'romanticism' – whose abuse has rendered it unfit as a title for the diverse Romantic period of the nineteenth century, so difficult to describe – is also inappropriate when the outward appearance of a new work of art seems to remind us of an older one.

A few years ago the discovery of melodics was a great enrichment of my means of expression; the very difficult process of simplifying my language, which was sometimes only possible by (seemingly) lowering standards, was accelerated by discovering the surprisingly active and contemporary nature of street-calls and canzonetti, *which are based around simple arrangements of intervals. In the place of serial tonal sequences, which on a purely superficial level guarantee a certain 'contemporary' quality, the simplest tone progressions would be used; their basic intervals, naturally connected with singing, would contain everything that needed to be said. Witness to this approach are various parts of the opera* König Hirsch *and then* Five Neapolitan Songs, *and from then on this newly found tonal valency, which had existed for years, began to flood into scores horizontally and vertically. Tension-building intervals such as seconds and sevenths regained their tension, once they were again viewed as sources of tension. Tonal colours, rhythms, chords and themes were invented on the way to the work's goal, their rules and construction coming from the figures expressed in the first bars, with their development and variation in no way subject to any external convention, responding only to the needs of the work. The rules lose their validity once the final bar of the work has been written.*

The longer one lives in a climate far from the Mediterranean, the more improbable its beauty appears in one's memory. And upon one's return, one finds it even more beautiful than one had remembered it. It is early spring; one sees a world in crystal glass, or in a kaleidoscope of pure light, new every day, unrepeatable. On the Via Carraciolo, the most elegant street, fishermen are spreading out their nets; a herd of goats is roaming; not far from here lies the Luna Park with its boorish cheer; one can hear the little ovens merrily whistling on the gaily illustrated carts of the peanut salesmen; old-fashioned steamers glide over the horizon, leaving a long trail of smoke behind them which stands still in the air; and in Mergellina one can wait in a café until the lights go on in the hills, lights that seem to stand out against the alabaster sky, and that later, when it has become quite dark, are reflected on the sea, like a chain of lanterns lit for the nightly octopus hunt.

The next work, the continuation of Act II, was made up of a number of mimes, which follow on from Beatrice's variations. She playfully dangles the amulet in the water, and Tirrenio's hand grabs it and pulls it down into the deep. Anger and dismay are the result, and one feels more strongly than before how close supernatural elements are, ready to interfere in the human world. 'Ondine' calls appear, and the nymph – currently being pulled this way and that between the human world and the water – tries her best to resist them. As a gesture of reconciliation and consolation towards Beatrice, Ondine reaches into the sea, pulls out a sparkling amulet made of coral and offers it to her. The reactions of fear and disgust are even stronger than before: Palemon rips the amulet out of Ondine's hand and casts it back into the sea.

Finale, in which Ondine returns to her own kind, while Tirrenio sets loose a storm in which the ship is wrecked: it begins with the new Tirrenio-call (whose first notes originate from the King of the Cherries), alternating between trombones and horns, echoing in the harps, and then

Pas de deux, Act III

Grand pas, Act III

returning in rapid motifs in a solo trumpet. Ever-new musical creations surround him, as well as fragments from previous scenes, whose meanings have been distorted by events in the meantime – the Ondine call as well, Palemon's song, but everything is torn away by the vehemence of rhythms that urge ever onwards. The frenzy finally ends with a fortis-simo *unison, into which the brass crashes discordantly. This was the tender tone with which Palemon greeted Beatrice in the first act; here he has become hard and brutal, yet with the same notes.*

Thus Act III begins. This time the previous notes have been trans-formed into a fanfare; their sound develops under extensive, almost recitative-like arches in the violins. The curtain opens; Palemon is alone and must stand by his earthly Beatrice; Ondine seems lost forever to him.

Who is Ondine? 'You should know', she once said to him, according to de la Motte-Fouqué, 'that there are beings in the elements, which look almost like you and which only seldom show themselves to you. The wondrous salamanders play and glitter in the flames; deep in the earth live the withered, treacherous gnomes; the forest dwellers, natives of the air, roam the woodlands; and in the seas and rivers live the race de-scended from the water-ghosts. In the echoing crystal vaults, through which the heavens look in with sun and stars, it is a beautiful life: tall coral trees with blue and red fruits shine in the gardens, one can wander over pure sea-sand and over beautiful, colourful mussels, and the flutes draw a secret, silver veil over the beauties of the old world, which today's world is no longer worthy of rejoicing over. Below, the noble monuments are resplendent, high and serious and beautifully bedewed; but the beings who live there are sweet and lovely to regard, for the most part more beautiful than people…'

But here is Palemon, fixed firmly to the Earth, on the eve of his marriage to Beatrice, a human being, a real entity. Lost! He thinks of Ondine, and because, as Proust says, 'la douleur est un aussi puissant modificateur de la réalité qu'est l'ivresse', *it seems to him 'as if a swan's sigh takes him up on its wings and carries him far away over land*

Masks, Act III

and sea, singing gracefully all the while. – 'Sound and song of swans', he had to say to himself over and over; that must surely mean death… and as he looked down on the waters they became like pure crystal, so that he could see right through them to the bottom. He was overjoyed at this, as it enabled him to see Ondine… Admittedly she was in floods of tears and looked much sadder than in happier times…'

At this point the 2/2 rocking movement returns to the music with an echo in the woodwind, and above it lies a faraway cantilena, *with the harps sometimes providing a counterpoint. Beatrice wakes Palemon from his immersion in thought, and the picture he has vanishes. Beatrice's happy-go-lucky 'earthly'* polacca *contrasts with the reminiscences from Ondine's shadow dance. Servants enter to light up the room, friends and well-wishers enter.* Pas de seize: *a piece for wind, harps, cellos, double bass and timpani, with the following movements: Entrée, (*allegro– adagio, *the latter for four solo* horns), Variation *(*allegro moderato, *for* woodwind), Variation *(*adagio, *for* horns, *then* allegro *for all brass)*, Coda *(*andante, *then* allegro brillante *for all wind, ending with a reprise of the Entrée). In this work all of the* grands sujets *of the Royal Ballet were to be given a chance to shine. The music is markedly different from the previous pieces, not only in its orchestration, but also in the fact that in both rhythm and form it conforms to certain ceremonies of the old* Grand Pas, *in order to allow uninterrupted, pure demonstration of* tours en l'air, fouettés, jetés, cabrioles, batteries *etc.*

Following a short, preparatory mime, the divertissement is a further opportunity for the dancers to display their art, this time for the company's younger members. Despite the demands for virtuosity inherent in its arrangement, it is less ceremonial, also owing to the fact that it is actually a pas d'action: *the appearance of the Neapolitan masks. A new colour is introduced here as well: solo piano. This divertissement – which at the start should have the subtitle* The Cat's Variations, *because the first seven notes of the famous* Cat's Fugue *by Domenico Scarlatti form the basis of the work – can also be played as a small piano concerto under the title* 'Jeux des Tritons'.

It begins with an introduction, in which the theme is expressed in various settings. Allegro brillante. *In the first 'number' (*pas de six*), in which the piano appears, the previous tempo remains. The trios and arpeggios of the solo part are accompanied by the main theme, which crosses the whole of the orchestra. In no.* II *(*pas de trois, 3/4, meno mosso*), the piano plays variations over the Scarlatti notes which continue freely, from which completely new material emerges, before going back to the start of the movement, which is then adopted by the* tutti. No.III *(*pas de trois II, 4/4, allegro assai*) brings us back to Scarlatti, which is then given the run-up to a new creation '*alla turca*', whose syncopated closure leads into no.IV (*pas de vingt–quatre, 3/4, più mosso*), a tight interplay between piano and orchestra, crowded and tense with chords.*

This is followed by the very lively movements (as it happens, they all progressed from one to the next with attaca *from the start): the first (V) for three girls, with an exaggerated violin cantilena, the next (VI) for a boy,* alla breve, *with a bright piano motif, the next (VII) for two girls, a mirrored motif of the Scarlatti notes leading to the formation of something new, carried at first by the flute, then by the solo instrument. Next comes a reprise of the 'alla turca' from no.III, which is now blared by the whole orchestra.*

*Then, somewhat softer, comes no.VIII (*pas de six*), a triplet movement in the solo instrument, interrupted sternly from time to time by an intervention from the orchestra, soon finding again the quick, urgent tone of the whole divertissement, before leading on to the coda (*pas d'ensemble*), a sinister waltz, whose theme is once again half made up of returning elements of the Scarlatti motif. At its climax are syncopations over the sounds of the guitar's six open strings, E, A, D, G, B, E; these suddenly cease, but the movements, to which the dancers have been inspired, continue without music. This is all repeated once more intensively, and then percussion instruments start beating minims against the 3/4 time of the waltz, seemingly causing it to buckle completely, until a newly arriving motif combines with it and drives it to the end in* accelerando.

This music could cause confusion among fans of intense music, just as it defies explanation among Palemon's evening companions, who were not expecting this exposition of Neapolitan dance. Not ones for surprises, and believing their dignity (or dignity itself) to be constantly in danger, they would have preferred a proper, ordered evening to the invasion of these powdered white masks, for which they perhaps have no reassuring explanation to hand. 'Brilliant', perhaps 'too brilliant', or 'dangerous', they would murmur accusingly, while the masks are already falling, and instead of cheerful *pulcinelli*, wild air- and water-ghosts, destructive elements, are filling the house with terror...

As with the liberated people who storm the city on the evening of the ancient ritual of the *SS. Madonna di Piedigrotta*, suddenly filling the streets and overrunning the squares as if in a riot, all rules are broken; fools' hats, plumes, moons and stars made of colourful paper, noisy instruments from pagan times, tambourines and trumpets take the lead, symbols of disobedience, of joyful devastation, crowned by triumphant fireworks above the water. A million voices join in the laughter of liberation. Pulcinella is in the theatre, ever victorious over death, with a song. Orlando's dream: fiery dialogues set above dull rumbles on the timpani; weapons shining golden; a chaotic passage of Rossini music; the dramatic scenes of characters falling from the heavens in the puppet theatre, before the enraptured faithful audience, who take sides, heckling menacingly, (Rinaldo has to interrupt, calm things down, explain himself, appeal for mercy for his character, represented by woodwind and brass), arguing passionately amongst themselves over which of the rosy-cheeked puppets with the staring black eyes was the praiseworthy character, and which was worthy of disgust.

Tirrenio enters the stage with wild leaps; masked as a courtier, he introduces himself with a minuet for woodwind and solo viola and then, as the light on the stage fades, the whole orchestra seems to dissolve itself into glissandi, tremoli and vibrati, quiet calls from the distance; after that, once again in minuet tempo, but rough and harsh, the reprise of a motif from the danse générale of Act I, initially only for woodwind, but then for all, in hard pulses. A sustained unison in the full orchestra follows, from which Tirrenio's call emerges. More and more tritons and nymphs rush in, accompanied by lively woodwind triplets, and they chase the people until Tirrenio's signalling call from Act I sounds out triumphantly. The circle is closed. It has become quite dark; Palemon returns, enchanted, worried by the palpable closeness of his unearthly loved one.

Palemon's gentle organ motif mingles with the three notes of the Ondine call, which is once again given a melodic continuation. Ondine approaches, accompanied by a variation of one of the secondary themes from the Act I love scene (the only one in the entire work), which has now become a strong complaint. Palemon falls at her feet.

This last meeting is composed as a passacaglia, a simple canto in the strings above the bass line, which constantly gains in strength. The music is already fully aware of the end, even though this last conversation between human and ghost is only just beginning; and logically enough, at the end of the passacaglia is the fatal kiss. The death has a sound, as has already been hinted at in the prelude to this last act, of a loud, painful cry, which then ebbs away quickly, leading to the final, quiet elegy: a serene theme, on whose horizon Palemon and Ondine are recalled only in distantly related tones, becoming ever more silent, vanishing.

The completion of the score marked the end of my work on *Ondine* for the time being, and I could apply myself to other works. A long time would elapse before the work's performance: the dancers had an American tour to prepare for, during which time they would scarcely rehearse. In all this time (after I had played the whole work through once) I heard almost nothing more from London, and knew only that Ashton was working furiously, and that a letter from Dame Margot told me things were progressing well. I found out that Ashton was playing a tape

Final scene

recording of the fully orchestrated music in the ballet studio, and that the dancers were learning their parts to this (rather than to the piano which we had used at the start), taking their impulses directly from the real sounds of the instruments. Since this tape had been available only after the completion of the Act I choreography, the choreographer had had to change a great deal: the sound of the piano part had often led to misleading conclusions being drawn, and incorrect accents being set. In July 1958 I saw the whole of Act I, and was able to express my thanks for the first time to Fonteyn, Somes, Grant, Ashton and all the others.

Later in the year, a month before the premiere on 24 October, I went up to London again and watched the rehearsals in order to learn the choreography by heart, and began with my orchestral rehearsals. Since *Ondine* would be opening the season at Covent Garden, and, it being the eve of the opening of Parliament, society's 'winter season', we had the use of the opera house for the whole day. Dance, orchestral and technical rehearsals alternated with one another from early morning until late at night. One might say we were living in the theatre. I had soon made friends with the musicians of the orchestra, who were very nice people. I remember the leader, Charles Taylor, especially fondly, but many other names and faces have stayed in my memory, along with my admiration at so many excellent solo performances of often difficult passages, among them pianist Margaret Kitchin, who played the Act III piano solo.

In the breaks between rehearsals we went to the underground canteen, where Pulcinelli and their make-up artists, nymphs clothed in old dressing gowns or cardigans, piano players, dark-skinned stage workers from some colony or other, production assistants, fauns, trumpet players and sea maidens queued up for tea. To get something stronger one had to go over to the *Nag's Head*, where in those days one competed to buy one's colleagues a drink. Wherever one stood or went, one met people who were involved with *Ondine*; every conversation revolved around it. The politeness that held sway in this opera house, the spirit of wholehearted cooperation, borne of mutual respect, all things that are actually nothing short of boring, led to the normal torment of stage fright being replaced by feelings of pleasant anticipation.

In all the rehearsals the dancers who were not involved in this ballet sat at the back of the stalls completely without jealousy – interested colleagues, ready to help. The opera house's younger choreographers, Cranko, MacMillan and Rodriguez, were present, members of a large family. Even Dame Ninette de Valois sometimes managed to escape from her sickbed in a Windsor clinic and appeared sporadically, giving a few words of advice and many good wishes. From time to time the silhouette of David Webster, the theatre manager, could be seen. Hilda Gaunt, the leader of rehearsals, sat behind me at rehearsals and checked that my tempos corresponded to those of the tape with which the dancers had rehearsed, until my rapport with the orchestra was such that I could keep an eye on the stage, to accompany the scene, leading and animating it. Sir William Walton came to each of my rehearsals, his presence instilling confidence and courage, and thus I too got to experience his well-known loyalty towards younger colleagues.

We scarcely noticed anything of the beautiful October sun outside, and the last days are filled with things that one remembers only at the last minute; one has barely a moment's rest, the telephone rings continuously. Friends come from Germany, Italy, Paris, one waits at stations and airports, when time allows. Here and there one squeezes in a party in Mayfair or South Kensington, where one suddenly meets the people from Antonio's ballet, not even knowing who the host is; one meets angry young men and also less disagreeable intellectuals from Chelsea with velvet trousers and sometimes ruddy beads, chinless record collectors,

Indian researchers with furrowed brows talking in vague terms, people who still expect something of expressionism, and then it's back to the theatre, where one realises that our work can no longer be changed – were one to have an idea here and there that would have provoked a change – for it has now all been transferred into the hands of the technicians, the lighting people, the musicians, into the movements of the dancers, and tomorrow it will be submitted to the judgement of the audience. de Nobili, followed by J.M. Simon, wanders through the tailors' workshops, the painters' rooms, covered with paint stains and cobwebs; on the night of the premiere they would have to be dragged by force from the stage, as even as the curtain is about to go up there is still a small shade of colour to change, a contour to be adjusted. Through the peephole in the curtain a worker shows me the Royal Box; it is high up on the left, under the unicorn. We are all calm, having wished each other luck.

Fonteyn enters the stage and begins, like everyone else, to take a few steps to warm up, and then stops. Her smile is no longer related to her surroundings; it lives now for the glare of the spotlights which shine from all directions, and the other dancers are also now far away in their own worlds, and one can no longer talk to them.

At exactly 7pm the stage manager sends me down to the orchestra pit, and a minute later the curtain goes up.